What Is ir

Written by Rozanne Lanczak Williams
Created by Sue Lewis
Illustrated by Patty Briles

Creative Teaching Press

What Is in Bear's Box?
© 2002 Creative Teaching Press, Inc.
Written by Rozanne Lanczak Williams
Illustrated by Patty Briles
Project Manager: Sue Lewis
Project Director: Carolea Williams

Published in the United States of America by:
Creative Teaching Press, Inc.
P.O. Box 2723
Huntington Beach, CA 92647-0723

CTP 3216

What is in Bear's box?

A ball!

What is in Bear's box?
A bat!

What is in Bear's box?
Buttons!

What is in Bear's box?
Bugs!

6

But what is in Bear's big box?

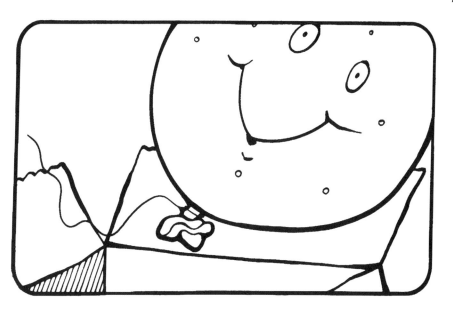

A balloon!

Bye-bye, Bear!

Create your own book!

Cover a single-serving cereal box with paper.
Add the title *What Is in _____'s Box?* Cut a
strip of blank paper to fit inside the box.
Accordion-fold the strip to make pages.
On each page write and illustrate an object
that begins with *b*. Glue one end to the inside
of the box.

Words in *What Is in Bear's Box?*

Initial Consonant: *b*
Bear's
Bear
box
ball
bat
buttons
bugs
big
balloon
but
bye-bye

High-Frequency Words
what
is
in
a